# DRINKING GAMES

TED LEECH

summersdale

# DRINKING GAMES

Summersdale Publishers Ltd
46 West Street
Chichester
West Sussex
PO19 1RP
UK

www.summersdale.com

Printed and bound in Great Britain

ISBN: 978-1-84024-701-5

# Contents

# Introduction

Most of these games have one thing in common: they combine a full glass of booze with making a complete fool of yourself – all the ingredients for a great night, in fact. These games take different formats (cards, chance, verbal, etc.) but the outcome is always the same… the players find themselves laughing hysterically at each other.

So gather your friends and crack open your favourite poison: here's a whole collection of ways to demonstrate your mental skills and dexterity and humiliate yourself in the grand name of fun!

# Drinking Penalties

Whenever you are instructed to drink in this book, you are expected to do so with moderation. To make things fair, it is best to decide on a set measurement for your drinking penalty. A good version is the 'two-finger rule' – where you hold two fingers to your glass and use that as a measure of how much drink to consume each time – but you can agree upon another amount between yourselves.

# International Drinking Rules

It's always fun to add some extra restrictions to keep people on their toes during an evening of fun. If you break any of the following rules, you must have a drink:

1. No pointing (you can use your elbows to gesture)

2. No swearing

3. You must drink with the hand that you don't normally use (e.g. your left if you are right-handed) and with your little finger pointing out.

# CARD
# GAMES

# The Ring of Fire

## You will need:
Three or more players, drink, an empty glass, a pack of cards

## How to play:
Everyone sits in a circle, with the empty pint glass in the centre. To make the 'Ring of Fire', spread the cards face down in a haphazard circle around the glass. Players then take it in turns to select a card from the Ring of Fire and turn it over. Each card signifies a different

drinking instruction which the player must follow ('take a drink' means drink one finger, unless otherwise specified):

**Black ace** – nominate another player to take a drink.
**Red ace** – player takes a drink.
**2–4** – follow the same pattern as above from two up to four fingers.
**5** – player puts their hand in the air. All the other players must do likewise: the last player to do so must take a drink.
**6** – player discreetly places their thumb on the table. All the other players must do likewise; the last player to do so must take a drink.
**7** – the player to their left must take a drink.

**8** – the player to their right must take a drink.

**9** – player says a word and each player around the circle must say a word that rhymes. The first player to hesitate or make a mistake must drink.

**10** – player nominates someone else to drink.

**Jack** – player must finish their drink.

**Queen** – everyone drinks 'to the Queen'.

**King** – player pours the remainder of their drink into the pint glass.

The player who picks up the fourth King must pour the remainder of their drink into the pint glass, then down its possibly rather dubious contents whilst standing on the table, as everyone sings 'Hey Baby'.

**Note:** if a player accidentally breaks the Ring of Fire at any point during the game, they must down their drink.

# Party Snap

## You will need:
Three or more players, drink, a pack of cards

## How to play:
The more players, the better. Nominate one person to be the dealer for the first round – the role then passes to the left after each round. The dealer begins by placing cards, face up, in a stack, calling out the number of each card as they do so. When two cards of the same number come up in sequence, the first person to bring their hand down

onto the top of the pile and shout 'Snap!' gets the top card, and then has the power to nominate a player to drink a number of fingers of their drink equal to the number of the card. A round ends when the dealer has no more cards.

# The Dictator Game

## You will need:

Three or more players, drink, a pack of cards

## How to play:

Each player takes a card. The player with the highest card is the dictator. The dictator then announces some rules: for example, even card = drink one finger of your drink, ace = down your drink. They then reshuffle the pack and deal five cards to each player, including themselves. For every card a player has that meets the dictator's rules, they have a drink, apart from the dictator, who instead nominates another player to take a drink. The dictatorship then passes to the left, and the new dictator announces their rules and deals. The dictator can, of course, change the rules as they see fit while they remain in power.

# Higher or Lower

## You will need:

Three or more players, drink, a pack of cards

## How to play:

Deal a card to the first player. They must guess whether the next card will be higher or lower. If the guess is incorrect, the player must drink a number of fingers of their drink equal to the value of the card, or finish their drink for a picture card. If the guess is right, or if the next card is the same as the current card, they get another go. If they survive up to three cards they may choose to continue or to pass to the next player.

Spice it up by allowing each player who guesses right three times in a row to make up a new rule. For example:

You're not allowed to cross you limbs
You must slap your thighs before drinking
You must say the opposite of what you mean

Players in violation of rules must, naturally, take a drink.
For players who aren't great with numbers, you could replace higher or lower with red or black.

# Cheat!

## You will need:
Up to six players, drink, a pack of cards

## How to play:
The object of this game is to get rid of all your cards. Sit in a circle, deal the cards evenly, and take it in turns to lay face down your aces, then your twos, etc. in a stack in the centre. Players may lay down cards of the same value or one higher than the previous person. If a player doesn't have any of either value of card, they must lie.

If someone thinks they are lying, they call out 'Cheat!' The accused player must then reveal their cards – if they were indeed lying, they must take as many fingers of their drink as the value of the card they claimed to be placing down (if it was a picture card they must finish their drink). If someone is wrongly accused of cheating, the accuser must drink the prescribed amount.

When the cheat or accuser has drunk their penalty drink, they must then pick up all the cards in that stack and add them to their own. The winner is the first player to discard all of their cards.

# Card Head

## You will need:

Three or more players, drink, a pack of cards

## How to play:

Players sit in a circle. Each player is dealt a card which they have to stick on their forehead without looking at. If you can't get the card to stay on your head hold it on with your finger. You'll be able to see the value of your fellow players' cards but you won't have any idea of what your own card is. The idea is to gamble as to whether you think your own card is higher or lower than that of your friends. If you take a bet and lose, you must have a drink. If you win, you may nominate another player to drink.

# Horse Races

## You will need:
Three or more players, drink, a pack of cards

## How to play:
Remove the aces from the pack and then lay five to ten cards face down in a row. This is the racing track: the longer the row, the longer the game will last. Place two of the aces above and two below the track, in line with the first card.

Players must then name the ace that they think will win, and bet a number of fingers of their drink. When all bets have been raised, the dealer takes the rest of the pack and turns over the top card. Whichever suit the card is, the ace of the same suit is moved forward one place along the track. The dealer continues in this manner until one ace wins the race by reaching the last card of the track.

The losers must drink the number of fingers they bet, and the winner can nominate any combination of the other players to drink their bet. For example, if they bet six fingers, they can give two fingers each to three other players, or all six fingers to just one player. Things can get pretty heated in the world of gambling so make a note of everyone's bets at the start of the game if you want to ensure no one tries to wriggle out of their wager.

# Across the Bridge

## You will need:
Two or more players, drink, a pack of cards

## How to play:
Deal ten cards face down in a row to form the bridge. Players take it turns to flip over a card. If they turn over a numbered card they're safe, and play passes to the next player. If they turn over a picture card or an ace, they must drink a finger of their drink

and add more cards to the bridge, depending on the card they turn over:

**Jack** – one finger, one card
**Queen** – two fingers, two cards
**King** – three fingers, three cards
**Ace** – four fingers, four cards

The game ends when all the cards on the bridge have been turned, or the pack runs out.

# Catch-22

## You will need:
Two players, drink, a pack of cards

## How to play:
Take the ace through to the Jack of both hearts and spades from a pack of cards (this should give you 22 cards). Put the rest of the pack to one side.

Each player chooses a suit and play begins. Player one takes the cards and throws them towards player two, who must try to catch as many as they can. The cards of each suit caught are then counted and both players must drink the same number of fingers as cards caught in their suit. Repeat ad nauseam.

You can add some extra rules to liven things up a bit:

**Add the Jokers in** – if they are caught, the players' suits are reversed.

**Add the Queens in** – if they are caught, the player throwing must drink for the total number of cards caught.

# Pyramid

## You will need:
Two or more players, drink, a pack of cards

## How to play:
Lay 15 cards out face down in the shape of a pyramid, with a row of five cards at the bottom, four on the line above and so on leading up to one card at the top.

Players take it in turns to turn over the cards one at a time starting from the bottom row and working upwards through the rows until they turn over a picture card or an ace.

Each of these cards comes with a drinking penalty:

**Jack** – one finger
**Queen** – two fingers
**King** – three fingers
**Ace** – four fingers

Once a player has revealed a picture card/ace and drunk the penalty, all the cards they have turned over so far are picked up, shuffled back into the pack and the gaps in the pyramid are refilled. The player must then start again. Play passes to the next player only when the first player has made it all the way to the top without having to take a drink or when a player has finished their drink.

# Beat the Dealer

## You will need:
Three or more players, drink, a pack of cards

## How to play:
First cut the cards to decide who will be the dealer. The dealer holds the deck and the player to their right tries to guess the rank of the card on top. Without revealing it, the dealer looks at the card and tells the player whether they are right, or if not, whether it is higher or lower than their guess. The

player is allowed one more attempt before the card is revealed.

They must then drink the number of fingers difference between their guess and the card's value. So, if their final guess was five and the card was an ace, they must drink four fingers.

If the player guesses the card right on their first go, then the dealer must drink six fingers, if they guess right on their second guess, then the dealer only has to drink three. Once three players have had a turn, the role of dealer passes to the next player clockwise.

The used cards are placed face up in numerical order, so that all players can see them. As more cards go out, it gets easier for players to guess correctly and beat the dealer.

# The Dealer and the Fuzz

## You will need:
Four or more players, drink, a pack of cards

## How to play:
Take from the pack one playing card per person. Within these there must be one King and one ace. Players sit in a circle and the cards are then dealt face down. Everyone takes a quick look at theirs. The person who gets the King is 'The Fuzz' and the person who gets the ace is 'The

Dealer'. The Dealer must very discreetly wink at one of the other players, who will after a delay say, 'the deal has been made'. At this time The Fuzz identifies themselves and tries to guess who The Dealer is. If The Fuzz chooses the wrong player they must have a drink. If they get it wrong again, they must drink the number on the wrongly accused person's card, for example, ten fingers for a ten of clubs. When The Fuzz finally chooses correctly, The Dealer has to drink the total number on the remaining cards. After this, the cards are shuffled, re-dealt and the game continues.

# Spoons

## You will need:

Three or more players, drink, a pack of cards, spoons

## How to play:

Take a set of four matching cards from the pack for each player. Players sit in a circle with the spoons in the centre (there should be one less spoon than there are players). The cards are then shuffled and four are dealt to each player. The aim of the game is to collect four of the same value card.

Everyone looks at their cards, then selects a card to discard and places it face down to their left and picks up the discarded card from the player on their right. This is repeated, the passing usually speeding up as the game progresses.

Once a player has four of a kind they must discreetly remove a spoon from the centre and then resume playing as before, but always discarding the card they have just picked up so that they keep their set of four.

The person who doesn't manage to grab a spoon loses and must down their drink and sit out the next round. Play starts again with one less set of cards and one less spoon and continues until only one spoon remains – the player who ends up with this is the winner.

# Go Fish

## You will need:
Two or more players, drink, a pack of cards

## How to play:
Each player is dealt five cards and the rest of the pack is roughly spread out in the centre. If any players have pairs in their hand they must discard them and take replacement cards from the pack. Player one begins by choosing a card in their hand and asking another player if they have any cards of that rank. If that player has any of the requested

card in their hand they must give them all to player one and drink two fingers of their drink if it's a numbered card, or three fingers if it's a picture card or an ace. Player one may then place the pair face up in front of them and take another turn. If player two does not have any of the requested card, they reply 'Go Fish' and player one must drink a finger of their drink and pick up another card from the centre. (If the card they select makes a pair with one in their hand, they may discard the pair, but play still passes to the next player.)

Whenever a pair is laid down, all the other players must drink two fingers of their drinks. Play continues clockwise until one player gets rid of all their cards. The winner is the player who has discarded the highest number of pairs when the game ends – and they can choose a suitable forfeit for the losers.

# GAMES
# OF
# CHANCE

# Nasty or Nice

## You will need:
Two or more players, drink, a coin

## How to play:
This is guaranteed to get everyone in the party spirit, and is best played in a bar that offers a good shooters menu to choose from, or at home with a selection of spirits. Order a variety of shooters from the bar, or, if you are at home, pour out some different shots. Make sure that there is at least one shot per person, and that about half of them

are shots that taste 'nice' (think Irish cream, Slippery Nipples, peach schnapps) and the other half are 'nasty' (think tequila, black sambuca, or anything with Tabasco in it). Each player takes it in turns to flip the coin, guessing first whether it will land heads or tails up. If they get it right, they get to drink a shot of their choice. If they get it wrong, the other players choose for them – and it's up to them to choose whether a 'nasty' or 'nice' shot is in order.

# The Flicks

## You will need:
Two or more players, drink, a coin, an empty glass

## How to play:
The object of this game is not to win or lose, merely to stay in the game. Essentially, all you have to do is to flick a coin on its flat side into the empty glass. Each player takes a turn at doing this, and when anyone succeeds they can nominate another person to drink two fingers. They must continue to

take flicks of the coin until they miss. When a player misses, they can have another attempt if they want, but a second failure is punished by taking a drink themselves.

When a player has scored three consecutive successful shots, they can nominate every other player to drink twice the agreed amount.

# Fifty-Fifty

## You will need:

Three or more players, drink, a beer mat

## How to play:

This is the simplest game *on the planet*, and therefore highly recommended for those who feel they are *off it*. Take a beer mat, and flip it into the air. If it lands face up, nominate someone to have some of their drink. If it lands face down, you have to drink. Each person takes it in turns to flip the mat, with a fifty-fifty chance of either having to have a drink or nominate someone else. The game works best if people conspire to nominate the same player to have a drink whenever they win. You had better hope that unlucky player isn't you!

# Dice

## You will need:
Two or more players, drink, a die, six plastic cups, a marker pen, a jug

## How to play:
Take the plastic cups, number them one to six with the marker and set them out in a row on a table. Fill the jug with beer, punch or another alcoholic beverage of your choice. Players take turns to roll the die. If a player rolls a number which corresponds with an empty cup, they can fill it with as much or

as little drink as they like. Play then passes to the next person. If the cup already has some drink in it, they must down the contents and then roll again. Remember when you're pouring drink into a cup that you could well be the person who ends up drinking from it!

# Sixes

## You will need:
Two or more players, drink, two dice

## How to play:
This game is simple but effective if you have a large amount of alcohol to work your way through.

Players take it in turns to roll the dice. If the numbers on the two dice add up to six (for example, a four and a two) or one of them is a six, the player must drink. If a player rolls a double, they must drink fingers equivalent to the number on one of the die – so if they roll a double four, they must drink four fingers. For a double three or six, both rules apply: a finger for adding up to six, and a number of fingers for the double. So a double six means eight fingers: two for two sixes, plus another six for rolling a double six.

# Mexicali

**You will need:**
Two or more players, drink, a cup, two dice

**How to play:**
Players take it in turns to shake the two dice in the cup and slam them down on the table. Without letting anyone else see, the player takes a peek at what they've rolled and announces their score. Rather than adding the dice to get a score, the two numbers are combined with the highest always coming first: for example, a three and a two would

make 32, four and a five 54. A two and a one, 21, is known as a Mexicali and beats all other combinations.

The aim is for each roll to be higher than the last person's; if it isn't, then players must bluff. When a player is accused of bluffing, they must reveal the dice: if they were lying they must take a drink, but if they were telling the truth, the accuser must drink. If a player is caught bluffing a Mexicali, they must down their drink.

Try adding your own rules. For example:

A 61 means everyone must take a drink
A 31 means the play changes direction

# Desperate to Drink

## You will need:
Three or six players, drink, a die

## How to play:
Everyone chooses a number between one and six, or two numbers each if there are only three players. The first player rolls the die: whichever number it lands on, the player who chose that number must take a drink. The die is only passed on to the next

player once the first player has rolled their own number and taken a drink. Continue until each player has had a turn at rolling the die, or until you run out of drink.

# Reckless

## You will need:
Three or more players, drink, a coin, an empty glass

## How to play:
Players sit in a circle, with the empty glass in the centre. Player one takes the coin and the person to their right must pour some of their own drink into the empty glass, then call heads or tails. The more reckless they are, the more drink they will pour into the glass. Player one then flips the coin: if the

other player has guessed correctly, they take the coin and play moves on, with the person to their right now adding to what's already in the glass. If they guess wrongly, they must drain the glass in the centre, and player one takes another turn at flipping the coin.

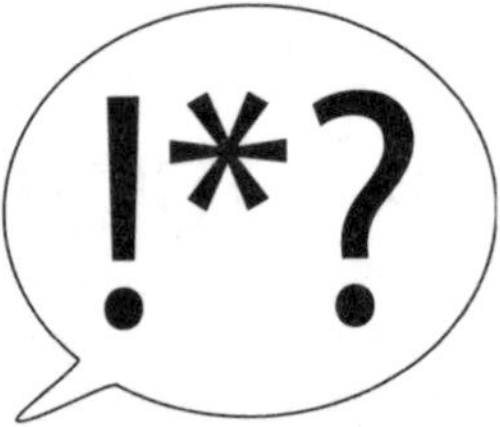


# VERBAL GAMES

!*?

# Twenty-one

**You will need:**
Four or more players, drink

**How to play:**
Everyone sits around in a circle. Any player can start the game by saying 'one'. The person on their left says 'two' and so on around the circle, continuing up through the numbers to twenty-one. Sounds pretty simple? Well, think again: there are a few rules to make things that little bit more interesting.

If a player says two consecutive numbers – for example, 'three, four' – play skips the player next to them and moves to the following player.

If a player says three consecutive numbers, the direction of play is reversed. This means that everyone has to pay very close attention; if a player makes a mistake, they must drink a finger of their drink.

The player who says twenty-one must down their drink and create a new rule to replace one of the numbers. Play then resumes from number one, and each time twenty-one is reached, a new rule is added. You can make the rules as silly or as complicated as you like. For example:

Instead of saying the number three, players must stand up and sing the first line of a well-known song.

Instead of saying the number five or any multiple of five, players must clap their hands and stamp their feet.

Instead of saying the number eight, players have to remove an item of clothing.

# The Celebrity Game

**You will need:**
Two or more players, drink

**How to play:**
Sit around a table. The first person turns to the person on their left and says the name of a celebrity. They then have to think of a celebrity whose name begins with the first

letter of that famous person's surname. For example, if the first celebrity named is Jennifer Aniston, the next one could be Angelina Jolie, and the next could be Jeremy Paxman, and so on. This continues around the table and the direction will only be reversed if someone says a name where the first letter of both the first name and the surname are the same e.g. Marilyn Manson.

The most important rule is that you must play this game without pausing. If you do pause you have to 'drink while you think', drinking continuously until you think of a person. If you say a name that has already been mentioned, you have to down your drink as a penalty.

!*?

# I Have Never

**You will need:**
Three or more players, drink

**How to play:**
Take it in turns to name something that you have never done. For example, 'I've never eaten a whole Toblerone in one sitting.' If any of the other players have done this thing, they must take a drink, so you can play to your advantage by saying things that you know the other players have done. However, if any of the others think that you are lying, they may say so and if they are

right, you have to down your drink. If they
are wrong the joke's on them and they have
to finish their own drink.

# Down at the Zoo

## You will need:
Three or more players, drink

## How to play:
Each player must choose an animal they would like to be during the game, and an action to go with it. Before play begins, everyone announces their type of animal, and demonstrates their action. For example, if they choose to be a lion they might roar,

and claw the air with one hand. The sillier you make your action the better. The first player does their action and that of any other player they choose. For example, the player who chose to be the lion would do their lion action, followed by that of another player, such as the reindeer. Play then passes to that player, who must do the animal action of the first player, their own action, and the action of another player. So, the reindeer would do the lion action, their own reindeer action, then the action of the next player they wished to pass to, and so on...

Play continues until someone makes a mistake and has to down their drink.

# Slap, Clap, Click

## You will need:
Two or more players, drink

## How to play:
This is one of the hardest games to play... those without a sense of rhythm will be in trouble! Before starting the game a category has to be decided, such as 'Animals' or 'Film Titles'. Players sit in a circle or around a table and begin the game by slapping their

thighs with both hands simultaneously, then clapping their hands together and finally clicking their fingers with their left and then right hand. This routine should build up into a steady four-beat rhythm that goes: slap, clap, click, click. Whilst the players are doing this they have to take turns to call out a word belonging to the category decided, keeping strictly to the rhythm by saying the word on the fourth beat, at the same time as the final click of their fingers. If a player fails to think of a word when the beat gets to them, loses rhythm or says a word that doesn't fit the category, they must have a drink.

# Who Am I?

### You will need:
Two or more players, drink, paper, a pen, some sticky tape

### How to play:
One player writes down the name of a famous person on a piece of paper and sticks it to the forehead of another player.

Everyone can see the name on the paper except the person on whose forehead it is stuck. This person must find out who they are by asking questions to each player in turn. Only 'yes' or 'no' may be given as answers. For every 'no' given the person asking the questions must take a drink.

# Sentence

## You will need:
Two or more players, drink

## How to play:
Someone starts with a word, any word. The next person has to say a word that could make a sentence with the word that has just been said, and so on.

The game goes on until someone says a word that doesn't make sense, or until someone hesitates, or until they laugh so much that they can't talk. This person then has to have a drink and the game continues. The sentences constructed when this game is played can become absolutely bizarre (and hilarious), especially if some of the players are lateral thinkers, but as long as the sentence makes grammatical sense it will count.

# Fuzzy Duck

## You will need:
Three or more players, drink

## How to play:
Players sit in a circle. The first person turns to their left and says, 'Fuzzy Duck'. The next person turns to their left and does the same. This continues until somebody turns to the person who's just said 'Fuzzy Duck' to them, and says 'Duzzy?' The question changes the direction and the phrase changes to 'Ducky Fuzz'. Anyone can reverse the direction by

saying 'Duzzy?', but each person may only do it twice per round. The idea is to go round as fast as you can. Stalling or getting it wrong means you have to have a drink. It's probably best not to play this one within earshot of your mother-in-law/ local priest/ young children; the game can result in some very rude words being thrown about!

!*?

# Animal, Vegetable or Mineral

**You will need:**
Two or more players, drink

**How to play:**
Take it in turns to think of an object that fits one of the animal, vegetable or mineral categories. The other players have three questions each, to which the person being

questioned must answer 'yes' or 'no'. (The first question should always be, 'Are you animal, vegetable or mineral?') If a player fails to guess correctly within three questions they must drink and the questioning moves to the next person. If a player's three questions are all answered 'yes', but without leading to a final identification, that player may continue to ask questions until they receive a 'no' or until they correctly identify the animal, vegetable or mineral.

# A, B, C

**You will need:**
Two or more players, drink

**How to play:**
Sit in a circle and choose a category; for example: films. Play starts with the letter A, with every player having to think of a film (or other word related to the chosen category) beginning with A. The first person might say 'Armageddon', the next 'All Quiet on the Western Front', with play continuing clockwise. If a player hesitates or can't think

of a word they must have a drink. Play then resumes with B, then C, until Z is reached, or everyone has had enough, or can no longer speak.

!\*?

# The Vegetable Game

## You will need:
Three or more players, drink

## How to play:
The aim of this game is to speak without showing your teeth. It may sound simple, but after a few drinks it's really not...

Each player chooses a vegetable name. Player one begins play by saying their own vegetable name and then calling another player. So, if they're a Cucumber and another player is a Pumpkin, they would say: 'Cucumber. Cucumber calls Pumpkin.' The player who is Pumpkin will then say: 'Pumpkin, Pumpkin calls Potato,' and so on.

If any player shows their teeth when speaking they must have a drink. You can make things trickier by inventing new rules. For example:

If someone shouts 'swap', everyone must swap names with the player opposite them.

Players can't call vegetables of the same colour, e.g. a Carrot can't call a Pumpkin.

!*?

# Whiz,
# Bounce, Boing

## You will need:
Four or more players, drink

## How to play:
This game requires a degree of mental agility, so play it at the start of an evening.

Everyone sits in a circle. Only three words may be spoken: Whiz, Bounce and Boing. Imagine that there is a ball: these words govern how the ball passes around the circle. Someone starts by saying one of the words:

**Whiz** – the imaginary ball passes to the next player

**Bounce** – the ball skips the next player and goes to the following player

**Boing** – the ball reverses direction

If a player makes a mistake they must drink until the others say 'stop'.

!*?

# Ibble Dibble

**You will need:**
Three or more players, drink, a cork, a lighter/matches

**How to play:**
First char the underside of a cork by lighting it, letting it burn and blowing it out. Be careful when doing this and let the cork cool properly before the game begins, as the cork will be used during play to make marks on players' faces. Any marks on the cheeks are called 'ibbles', whilst marks on the forehead are called 'dibbles'. Establish a

numbered playing order which you will stick to throughout the game.

Play begins with player one calling out the following:

'This is Ibble Dibble Number One with no ibbles and no dibbles calling Ibble Dibble Number [insert chosen player's number] with no ibbles and no dibbles.'

The chosen player must then respond:

'This is Ibble Dibble Number [insert number] with no ibbles and no dibbles calling Ibble Dibble Number [insert yet another player's number] with no ibbles and no dibbles.'

The game continues in this way until a player makes a mistake or speaks out of turn: they must then take a drink and receive either an ibble or dibble on their face. When play resumes, the other players must remember to name their ibble/dibble when they call them. For example, if player Number Two made a mistake and was marked on the cheek, the game would continue:

'This is Ibble Dibble Number Two with one ibble and no dibbles calling Ibble Dibble Number [insert chosen player's number] with no ibbles and no dibbles.'

# SILLY AND MESSY GAMES

# The
# Sinking Ship

## You will need:
Two or more players, drink, a pitcher, an empty glass

## How to play:
This nerve-wracking game will have you holding your breath as the tension mounts: be prepared to get covered in booze at some point! Each player should have their own full glass of drink at the beginning of the

game. Sit around a table, with the semi-full pitcher in the centre. Put the empty glass, upright, into the pitcher so that it floats. You may need to pour a small amount of drink into the bottom of the glass before play commences to give it some stability. Each player then takes it in turns to pour some of their own drink into the floating glass, then wait a few seconds to see whether the glass sinks or not. Play continues in this manner until the glass sinks. The unlucky player who causes this to happen must fish the glass out from the bottom of the pitcher and down its contents.

# Gargle-Gurgle

## You will need:
Three or more players, drink

## How to play:
Each player takes it in turns to perform a song for their 'audience'. The catch is that songs cannot be sung – they must be gargled! The other players take turns to identify the song, and each incorrect guess is punished by a drinking penalty. If, after a second gargled

rendition, none of the players can guess the tune, the performer must finish an agreed quantity of their drink.

# Musical Chairs

## You will need:
Four or more players, drink, a CD player, chairs

## How to play:
Arrange the chairs in a circle facing outwards, making sure there is one chair less than the number of players.

One person acts as the DJ and plays some music while the players walk around the chairs with their drinks in their hands. When the music stops they must all try to sit down. Whoever fails to get a seat must down their drink, and is out of the game. If anyone spills their drink in the scramble they must take a drink, but continue into the next round. Remove a chair and repeat, losing one person and one chair in each round until there is an eventual winner.

# Name That Tune

## You will need:
Three or more players, drink, a CD player

## How to play:
One person is the DJ, and the others take turns to identify songs within the first five seconds. If a song is incorrectly guessed, the player must have some of their drink. A player can choose to attempt identification in less than five seconds, subject to the

following drinking penalties if they get it wrong:

**A wrong guess at four seconds** – two fingers

**A wrong guess at three seconds** – three fingers

**A wrong guess at two seconds** – four fingers

**A wrong guess at one second** – the entire drink

# Sardines

## You will need:
Four or more players, drink, somewhere to hide

## How to play:
Everyone starts the game with a full glass of drink. One person hides with their drink somewhere and the other players must search for them. When someone finds them, they must have a drink from their glass, and join them in the hiding place. When someone finds them both, they must

both drink from their glasses, and all three people now hide, and so on. The last person to find the hideaways must take a number of gulps of their drink equal to the number of people concealed in the hiding place.

# Follow My Lead

## You will need:
Three or more players, drink

## How to play:
This is a copy-cat game, but instead of a 'Simon says…' instruction, the players must deduce by observation the action they must copy. Any player may choose to do an action at any time. For example; someone might decide to put their thumb on their forehead,

and everyone has to follow suit. The last person to catch on has to have a drink.

# Snakes and Ladders

## You will need:

Two or more players, drink, a snakes and ladders board game

## How to play:

Play a straightforward game of snakes and ladders, but with the following drinking instuctions:

**Up a ladder** – this player nominates an opponent to drink.

**Down a snake** – this player must have an agreed quantity of their drink.

At the end of the game, the loser must down whatever is left of their drink.

# Finger It

## You will need:
Three or more players, drink, an empty glass

## How to play:
Place the empty glass in the centre of a table and sit in a circle around it. Each player places a finger on the rim of the glass and one by one everyone bets how many fingers they think will be left on the glass. As soon as the last bet is called, players must very quickly lift their finger off the glass, or leave it where it is. Everyone must move immediately or

not at all – if anyone is suspected of changing their mind to help them win their bet, they will be given a drinking penalty.

If anyone has bet correctly they are 'safe' and may stop playing. All the other players put their fingers back on the rim and bet again. Play continues until there is only one person left: this player is the loser and must down their drink.

# Drunken Jenga

## You will need:
Two or more players, drink, a Jenga set, a pen

## How to play:
Take some of the Jenga blocks and write on them drinking instructions of your choice. For example:

Drink one finger
Drink two fingers
Nominate another player to drink
Finish your drink

Everyone drinks
All girls drink
All guys drink

Play the game as normal, players taking it in turns to remove a block. If they successfully draw out a block that has something written on it, they must follow the instruction. If the player knocks the tower over, they must finish their drink.

# Boat Race

## You will need:
Four or more players, drink, plastic cups

## How to play:
Be warned: things can get really messy with this game! You need an even number of players for this game, and the more the better. If you have an odd number, one person can act as the referee. Divide into two teams and line up on opposite sides of a long table. Each player will need a cup filled with drink – make sure the cups are all the same size and filled to the top.

On the count of three, the first player on each team starts to drink. Once they've drained their cup, they slam it upside down onto the table, which is the signal for the next player in their team to start drinking. If a player spills any of their drink, or turns their cup over before completely finishing it, their cup is refilled and they have to start again. The same goes for any overly keen player who starts drinking prematurely when the player before them hasn't yet finished. The winning team is the first to have all its members finish drinking. They may then choose a forfeit or drinking penalty for the losing team.

# Pass the Buck

## You will need:
Three or more players, drink, a CD player, a coin

## How to play:
This game is similar to pass the parcel, but requires much less preparation.

Everyone sits in a circle except for the DJ, who is responsible for playing and stopping the music.

Players must pass a coin around the circle. Whoever is holding the coin when the music stops must have a drink. If two people are touching it, mid-exchange, they must both drink.

# Racing Demon

## You will need:

Three or more players, drink, a die, a selection of old clothes (scarf, coat, gloves, pair of trousers, etc.)

## How to play:

Sit in a circle. Place the clothes and a glass of booze in the centre. Each player takes it in turn to throw the die. When a player throws a six they must run to the centre of the circle, put on all the clothes and drink from the centre glass. They must continue drinking until another player throws a six and replaces them. This can be quite a rowdy one – and you'll probably need to top up the centre glass fairly frequently!

# The After Eight Mint Game

## You will need:
Two or more players, drink, After Eight mints, shot glasses

## How to play:
Each player takes an After Eight mint and pours themselves a shot of alcohol. At the word 'Go!' players must place the After

Eight mints on their foreheads and, with their hands behind their backs, attempt to get them into their mouths without using their hands. If a player drops their mint, they must down their shot. Play continues until you run out of After Eight mints.

# Wibbly Wobbly

**You will need:**
Four or more players, drink, a garden or other outdoor space, sticks

**How to play:**
This game is guaranteed to make you feel very merry and possibly a little queasy. Divide into two equal teams. Insert two waist height sticks with blunt ends (we don't want any reports of eyes being gouged out!) into the ground at one end of the garden. Make sure that they are level with each

other and about two metres apart. Line up in your teams at the other end of the garden, each team opposite a stick. Ensure that both teams are the same distance from their respective sticks by marking a line on the ground and getting them to stand behind the line.

At the word 'Go!', the team member at the head of each line must run as fast as they can to the stick opposite their team, balance their forehead on the tip of the stick so that their eyes are facing the ground, then maintain this position as they spin around the stick a pre-agreed number of times. Each player must then run back to their team, and the next team member sets off to do the same.

The first team to have all members complete this (without falling over or puking) wins, and the other team have to down their drinks. This can last for as many rounds as you like. Try changing the number of spins required on each round to add to the chaos and confusion.

# TV Drinking

**You will need:**
Two or more players, drink, a TV

**How to play:**
Choose your favourite TV show and invent some rules that dictate when players should drink. For example:

> *The Simpsons* – everyone drinks each time Homer says 'D'oh'
>
> *EastEnders* – everyone drinks each time there is a scene in the pub

**James Bond films** – everyone drinks each time someone attempts to kill James Bond

# Vodka Roulette

## You will need:
Two or more players, drink (vodka or other clear spirit), shot glasses, water

## How to play:
Fill as many shot glasses as there are players with water, except for one, which is filled with vodka. Mix up the glasses and hand out the shots. Everyone must down their shot at the same time: whoever gets the vodka (the person with an unhappy look on their face

and probably demanding a glass of water!) loses and is out of the next round. Repeat until there is one player left: they are the winner and can choose a drinking penalty for the other players.

# The Peanut Race

**You will need:**
Two or more players, drink, a bag of peanuts

**How to play:**
Each player drops a peanut into their own full glass at exactly the same time when someone shouts 'Drop!' The peanut will sink to the bottom, then rise up again.

The player whose peanut comes to the surface last is the loser, and must drink their entire glass. The loser's glass is then refilled and another round is played. After a round each player must retrieve the peanut from their glass, eat it, and choose a new one.

# Magic Penny

**You will need:**
Drink, friends, a coin

**How to play:**
You can play this with a penny or a bottle top, but an edible item such as a peanut might be more advisable in case of accidental swallowing. Whatever your chosen item, it becomes the 'Magic Penny' for the duration of the game. This is something you can play over the course of an evening. Someone begins play by announcing to the group:

'The magic penny is now in play.' If someone is holding a drink in their hand and the person holding the Magic Penny manages to slip it into their glass, they have to down their drink. If you drop the Magic Penny in someone's glass when they are not holding it, or you throw it at their glass and miss, you must down your target's drink and buy/ pour them another one. The power of the penny passes to the person who receives it in their glass – once they have downed their drink they may target another player.

# Tree House

**You will need:**
Three or more players, drink

**How to play:**
This can be played at home or on a pub crawl when walking between pubs. The rules are simple: if someone shouts out 'Tree house!', everyone must get up off the ground and the last person to do so must down their drink. If you are playing the game between pubs, the last person has to buy the next round of drinks.

# Sixty Seconds

**You will need:**
Two or more players, drink, a clock/watch

**How to play:**
This is the easiest game in the book. Each player picks a number from one to twelve. When the second hand passes a player's chosen number, they take a drink.

www.summersdale.com